MONSTRUM POETICA

Published by Raw Dog Screaming Press
Bowie, MD
First Edition

Book design: Jennifer Barnes
Cover art copyright 2021 by Steven Archer
egolikeness.com

Printed in the United States of America
ISBN: 978-1-947879-35-5

Library of Congress Control Number:
2021938977

www.RawDogScreaming.com

Praise for *Monstrum Poetica*

"*Monstrum Poetica* gives fascinating information on little-known fiends then offers accompanying poems that bring these monsters to life, terrifying verses that make us want to hide in a corner and plea for mercy."
– Elizabeth Massie, author of *Sineater, Hell Gate,* the *Ameri-Scares* series

"For those who appreciate dark poetry, herein is a tasty dish of disturbing poems, thanks to the language skills of an accomplished word-monger. Each and all, terrifyingly original. Wolfe provides a variety of forms (concrete, free verse, etc.) as well as monsters of all sort. She includes some from folklore, others more common to Western pop culture like werewolves and vampires."
– Marge Simon, multiple Bram Stoker Winner, Grand Master poet, SFPA

"Just as much a dark, lyrical vision as a field guide to things that go bump in the night. There are monsters in this collection that will not leave you alone. There are turns of phrase that will do the same. You didn't think you could get truly scared from a poem? Think again."
– Josh Malerman, *New York Times* best-selling author of *Bird Box* and *Unbury Carol*

"Wondrous, dark, and full of the dread that makes us remember why we look over our shoulders when walking in unknown territories, this collection is one that lingers in the best possible way. I was told to expect great things from Jezzy Wolfe and I was not disappointed!"
– James A. Moore, author of *Boomtown* and the Seven Forges series

"...a wondrous journey through some of the world's most famous and infamous creatures and folklore. This is a book to keep on the bookshelf–to explore its mysteries and enjoy its poetic forms again and again. Loved it!"
– John Palisano, Bram Stoker Award-Winning author of *Ghost Heart*, President of The Horror Writers Association

"Drenched with thrilling darkness, Jezzy Wolfe's *Monstrum Poetica* is full of the wonderful worst. Monsters of all shapes, sizes, shades and orientations populate her pages to haunt and delight. Wolfe explores a variety of poetic forms from fantastic shape/concrete poems to well-constructed free verse. For those that love monsters, *Monstrum Poetica* is a beautiful monster manual of verse–a well-orchestrated symphony of the horrific to scream to."
– Angela Yuriko Smith, author of *The Bitter Suites* and *Dark Matters*, publisher and editor at *Space & Time Magazine*

"Wolfe creates fables in this collection, using shapes and spaces to make a roadmap to order, chaos, and the un-making of the familiar; inserting nightmares into wakening moments through an uncanny, beautiful mixture of images."
– Linda D. Addison, award-winning author, HWA Lifetime Achievement Award recipient and SFPA Grand Master

"*Monstrum Poetica* is an unholy pact with the reader, making us succulent prey of the blackest creatures from literature, mythology, urban legends and folklore. Wandering the charcoal dunes of the pages, with their starving long shadows, we'll find the ancestral wells of our memories."
– Bram Stoker Award & SFPA Elgin Award- winning author Alessandro Manzetti

MONSTRUM POETICA

by Jezzy Wolfe

RAW DOG
SCREAMING
PRESS

This book is dedicated to my mother, who taught me to love books, poetry, and fairy tales. Thank you for all those walks to the library, and all those books in our attic that I treasure to this day. Thank you for every time you sang me through thunderstorms and every time you bought me ice cream on those hot summer afternoons. Thank you for...everything. I am the woman I am because of you, and you will always be in my heart. I love and miss you forever, Mom.

Table of Contents

Introduction

We all love to be scared. Even if we don't consider ourselves fans of the horror genre, we like chills. Maybe it's scary movies around Halloween. Maybe it's skydiving or an escape room or campfire tales. No matter which form it takes, we love to be unnerved. Frequently or occasionally.

Most of us are superstitious, too, even if we don't think we are. I've seen self-proclaimed skeptics knock on wood or toss salt over one's shoulder. We talk about 'beginner's luck', we don't walk under ladders, and when a couple of bad things happen, we assume there will be one more unfortunate occurrence because those things come in threes.

We also tend to find a deep appeal in the abnormal, the strange, the weird. Oddball trivia, urban legends, stories about Bigfoot and the Loch Ness Monster.

None of this is a flaw in our character. It's who we are.

We are also a storytelling species. We share favorite tales, we whisper down the lane, we read, we watch TV or films. Stories are as old as our culture and likely older. Oral histories, ancient songs, and poetry predated the written word by thousands of years, and most of these forms of storytelling–spoken, sung, or written–contain elements of the fantastic, the religious, the superstitious, and the mystical. From The Epic of Gilgamesh, Enmerkar and the Lord of Aratta, the Pyramid Texts of Egypt, to the stories of holy books like the Bible, the Quran, the Hindu Vedas and Upanishads, and the oral storytelling of every culture from the Navajo to the Aboriginal tales of the Dreamtime.

For someone like me–a professional writer of horror in fiction as well as nonfiction, an editor of horror anthologies, an executive producer on a TV show and a movie based on my own horror writing, and writer of horror comics–I love the many varieties of horror storytelling. A personal favorite, though, is a form I do not write in.

Poetry.

I've always loved horror verse. Always. Since long before I even considered writing horror professionally. When I was young, I discovered the dark Gothic poems of Edgar Allan Poe, the cosmic horror of H.P. Lovecraft, and works of elegant strangeness by Robert Graves ("A Child's Nightmare"), Siegfried Sassoon ("Haunted"), Mary Elizabeth Coleridge ("The Witch"), John Keats "La Belle Dame Sans Merci"), Conrad Aiken ("The Vampire"), Edna St. Vincent Millay ("The Little Ghost"), Paul Laurence Dunbar ("The Haunted Oak"), Mary Howitt ("The Spider and the Fly: A Fable"), Robert Frost ("Ghost House"), Thomas Hardy ("The Shadow on the Stone"), Robert Herrick ("The Hag"), Robert Burns ("Halloween") and so many others.

It is my habit to read poetry aloud before I start my day's writing. I read poetry aloud when in hotels on book tour. I've read it many times in public–often shifting between works published as poetry and lyrics with unnerving qualities, such as Tom Waits' "Black Wings" and "Murder in the Red Barn." Years ago I ran a writers center in Bucks County, Pennsylvania, and hosted Beatnik Jazz Poetry slams. I've bought poetry for some of the anthologies I've edited for adults and teens. I'm on the board of the Horror Writers Association, an organization that annually presents its Bram Stoker Awards, including one for dark poetry. And now, among the other hats I wear, I'm the editor of Weird Tales Magazine, a century-old journal that launched the careers of writers like Lovecraft and Robert E. Howard and others. Although I am not a poet, I am an aficionado of it and a lifelong devoted fan of the form.

Which brings me to this book.

It's always a delight when I discover a new poet whose star is on the rise. Jezzy Wolfe's *Monstrum Poetica* is her first book of poetry. The poems are short, more like daggers than swords, and they pierce the heart and the mind. They are dark and witty, insightful and dreadful.

They also touch two other aspects very dear to my heart: folklore and urban legends. So far, I have written five nonfiction books about supernatural predators from around the world and throughout history. It's a passion engendered in me by my grandmother, who was what you might imagine Luna Lovegood (from the Harry Potter novels) as an old lady. Folkloric monsters are often much scarier and far stranger than the Hollywood versions.

Jezzy taps into that darkness with her poems. You will not find Disney's sanitized and romanticized mermaids here. She also touches on urban legends like the Mothman and the Black-Eyed Children. Ms. Wolfe likes to go dark, and with these poems she has, in fact, turned out the lights. She has clearly paused to listen to the voices in the shadows.

With the poems in this volume, you'll find werewolves and zombies, vampires and hungry ghosts, doppelgängers and hellhounds. And also creatures you might not have heard of before, but which you'll remember after reading.

These poems can be read in the silence of your room, or you can read them aloud, as I do, to entertain whoever–or whatever–might be listening. These are fine poems and they introduce a compelling new voice to the genre of dark verse. I have no doubt they will conjure strange images in your mind as they have done mine.

–Jonathan Maberry
New York Times bestselling author of *V-Wars* and *Rot & Ruin*

Aswang

In the Philippines, there are many monsters that exist in the vast island nation, but the most notorious and most feared are the *aswang*. An aswang is an evil shapeshifter and can appear as one of five beings: a vampire, witch, werewolf, ghoul, or a viscera sucker. These horrific beasts feed on the blood and fluids of humans. They are, more often than not, depicted as women who appear human by day, and shift into their aswang form at night to hunt and feed.

The most notorious of these is the *manananggal*. She is a self-separating viscera sucker. By day, she is quiet and reserved, her eyes always bloodshot from lack of sleep. At night, she grows bat wings and tears her torso from the lower half of her body so she can fly about and hunt prey. She hovers outside windows and uses her long proboscis tongue to suck the viscera and organs out of her victims, who are frequently pregnant women and fetuses. It is said that if one were to find the lower half of her body, and sprinkle it with salt or various other spices, she would be unable to reattach her torso and would die in the sunlight. Some say the manananggal are not actual aswangs, as much as a subspecies of aswang, but regardless, they are truly terrifying.

Sigbin are bizarre monsters that vaguely resemble the western chupacabra. They are described as having the similar body of a goat but without horns, paired with two huge ears that can be clapped like hands, and a long whip of a tail. They walk backwards with their head between their legs. What is unique about them is that sigbin are also blood suckers…only, they have the ability to suck that blood from the victim's shadows, a skill most chupacabras would surely find enviable. While the sigbin is distinctly different from weredog aswang, it is believed they are the pets of aswang.

The *amalanhig* is a zombie vampire aswang...basically, an aswang that died before passing its monstrous power on to a family member. As a result, it returns from the dead to bite the necks of humans. They chase pretty much anyone they encounter, and if they catch them, they will not only bite them, but tickle them to death, too. Yes. The amalanhig is apparently a tickle monster. They are said to be incredibly fast, so it is impossible to outrun them, unless one climbs a tree or crosses a bridge, as amalanhig are afraid of water. One could also run in a zig zag pattern because these creatures are stiff legged and can only move in a straight line. Despite the somewhat comical description of amalanhig, however, they can also mimic the voices of their victims...a rather creepy way to shock someone still.

Stories of the aswang date back as far as the sixteenth century and are often connected to the island of Panay, in the province of Capiz.

Ang Siya Na Masama

To the call of the *Tik Tik...*
Run.

Among banana tree roots,
the groves hide legs
that lay between the
under;
You will find it there.

Save yourself.
Save your village.

Find
discarded appendages
that wait in the muck of dark.

Bring salt.

Because
somewhere else
this bat-winged pain
with
hypodermic tongue...

Dances through cavities,
eviscerates membrane,
and relishes the sweet
viscera nectar
of
Mother's belly.

Mabangis na halimaw

The sky terror with
tendrils of entrails
writhing below...

> Always hungry.
> Always hunting.

Search for the severed body
and lace the wretched flesh
with spice
before she finds herself again.

For
Manananggal feasts
until all that remains is
decay
> and
> dry rot.

The *Tik Tik* is calling again.

Bring salt.

Chased

With wooden spines, the
stiff undead walk the most
rigid lines…the failure
of the After to hold rotted
revenants in their graves.
Forced to return, forced
to feed, chasing a vein for
the nectar of its pulse. Putrid
flesh draped like webbing
from bone chandeliers as
they hunt succulent prey
in the thicket. Steps clumsy.
Legs dead straight. Limbs
taut. Tongue pointy and
desirous to tickle arteries.
Tickle those rattling ribs.
Death comes with a laugh

or a scream but be assured,

it will come quickly. Find

a bridge or find a tree, trace

your footsteps with a Z. For

when their destination cannot

be twisted, twisting yours

may save your
soul.

Dog Deadly

It lurks
  deep behind,
distantly beside,
a corner creeper,
a clandestine
feeder.

  Its head
    hung between
its backward feet,
its whiplash tail,
ears that clap
warnings.

In the spaces between
the light, a covert nightmare
with its hungry tongue, searches

    for the boundary of shadow–
    for the edges of silhouettes–
    for the outlines of darknes–

Among spectral promises of bloody
draught, it pursues the copper
of exsanguinated flesh.

Cryptid
carnate canine,
hideous hound,
this nasty mongrel
    stalking its
    Prey.

A beasty
hovers just
beyond sight.
Evil incarnate
watches the
Light.

Black-Eyed Children

Black-eyed children are creatures that look like children between the ages of 6 and 16, that are pale skinned with unnatural black eyes concealed beneath the hat of their hoodie. Most reports describe them as quiet yet insistent, approaching people while in their cars or knocking on front doors, asking for a ride, or simply to be let in. Those encountering them experience a growing unease and dread, an almost hypnotic trance that tries to will them into compliance. Once the victim says *"no,"* the children become angry and demanding, pulling back their hoods to reveal those chilling eyes. Individuals would then encounter a variety of calamities, that range from power outages and electromagnetic disturbances, to physical dangers such as frequent nosebleeds and even deadly cancers.

There are no witnesses to what happens if someone says *"yes"* to the children. Everyone who ever meets them knows, instinctively, whatever follows will be bad.

Stories of the black-eyed children first circulated in 1996, detailing encounters with two unusual boys in Abilene, Texas. Afterwards, similar claims were made in Portland, Oregon. In 2014, new stories of the black-eyed children surfaced in the UK, primarily in Cannock Chase, an area of woodlands known to be a hotspot of supernatural activity. Witnesses there say the sightings of such children date back as far as the 1980s.

Some theories mention the possible connection between the black-eyed children, Men in Black, and extraterrestrial beings, since most incidents have occurred in areas where there are also heavy amounts of UFO sightings.

Beware the Children

The Otkon visit me often:
>   quiet knocks on my front door,
>   gentle taps on car windows,
>   small pleas with small voices.

Timid children in distress
tugging at my sympathy
like tiny fists on hoodie sleeves.

Until my eyes meet
the stares of the eyeless,
my veins run ice cold,
dead dread and panic.

I close my doors...
>   my windows...
>   and my ears

Those small voices become
>   the deep and dark
>   demands
of demons that wander
the desolate streets past sundown

disguised as innocence
with the palest skin
and the blackest souls.

The Road to Abilene

Downtown,
in the middle of Nowhere.
Texas forgotten...
Facades decayed and
silenced.
This town isn't home
        to anyone
        anymore...

A population missing,
windows black
and full of faded memories
of gingham curtains
and hot fruit pies,
blue noon skies and
        busy streets.

But that was the time
before they came.
Back before
one opened their doors
to desperate voices.

No one knew
better.
One by one
they offered help,

and
    one by one
they disappeared.

A town
    vanished
in a season's span,
victims of a plague
disguised in hoods
    and black eyes.

Victims of something
never spoken.

Main Street crumbled,
population 237,
all those forgotten
in idyllic Americana,
back when the whitewash was fresh.

Back before black eyes preyed on
    small town

    Nowhere.

Zeta Grey

Those aren't children
    …look at their eyes.
Those empty onyx orbs
do not hold a child's soul.
What they mirror is half human
    and less soul than synapse.
    A cocktail of mere
    mortal/alien blood
in carefully articulated costume.

Would I know if I peered into eyes
less human than mine?
    Would you?

Do we see ourselves
in something unearthly?
In camouflaged trickery?

If we can agree some faces
    are imposters, masked,
does it posit that the
children with black eyes
revisit us, rebranded as men in
    dark suits and pale skin,
    with black sunglasses that
    cover the same onyx orbs
of their most innocuous design?

What happens to those
    who obey demands falling

from unfamiliar mouths?
Does credulous compassion
predicate their complete undoing?
Will their blood be shed in fury
    or for the furtherment
    of a humanity on a hell
    bound trail of abolition?

Are those the black eyes
of savages,
    or saviors?

Perhaps our challenge is
to answer
    the children's calls,
to allow them over thresholds
and accept what that brings.

Maybe all they need is the
    taste of what it is to
    be human and wanting
    and delicate...or maybe
they need our blood for starseeds...

Never once ours, and not all theirs.

Bubáks

Every culture has its story of the bogeyman, that demonic visitor that sneaks in during the night to punish children who misbehave. Sometimes the punishment is being drowned in a nearby river, sometimes it is to disappear forever, and sometimes it is a grisly death. Parents employed the classic bogeyman tale to keep unruly children in line, and through unmitigated fear, it usually did the trick.

The *bubák* is one such creature, renowned in Czech and Slovenian folklore. Often depicted as a scarecrow, it wears a heavy black coat that hides the body of a skeleton underneath. The bubák can imitate the cry of a baby to wake its intended victim and lure them into the night. There, naughty children may be eaten, or secreted in the sleeves of its coat and kidnapped.

Legends say on the night of a full moon, the bubák weaves the souls of the children it kills into a cloth, before escaping to the Underworld on a cart pulled by black cats.

Bogeyman

On midnight winds,
the cries of a distant
infant
reach for the ears of
the young misbehaved.

So if you travel
by the full moon's light,
stay away from
stray carts and black cats.

Beware
the boundary betwixt
the mortal and the lost,
the satin curtains parted
to lure and to kill.

With a coat full of bones
and the bodies of children,
The bubák is waiting
to vanquish their souls.

Watching the Wait

The crows don't care—
They perch on his arms
and laugh at the children
    stumbling into
a corn-maze conundrum.

Falling at the feet of the
frightening field fellow,
the laughter rankles
the black bastions
    and the beast.

After midnight,
each child wakes
to gentle night calls from
the beckoning stranger
through the corn maze,
by the water's edge.

Tucked into the lapels
and sleeves of his coat,
the children vanish,
their laughter silenced in silk,
their bright eyes forever
dark.

Maybe tiny bodies will be found
lifeless and cold by the river,
coarse-skinned and baked brown
like dead corn husks in the fields.

No one
thinks to count.

The town mourns
their loss of tomorrow.
Across the sleeves of the straw man
laughing at the townsfolk,
the crows
don't
care.

Wirry-Cow, LLC

Tonight, the woods rattle
with Bugbears and Sack Men–
with the Babaroga and Kkullas.
They come collecting the
souls of spoilt youth,

with bags full of brats
satchels of sullen
knapsacks from the
disobedient brood...

Each
child meets their fate through
bumps in the night, their kicks
and screams muffled
by eternal reproach.

Under the fullest moon,
the sinister scarecrow
sits in his cat-drawn cart,
pulling souls like thread
into the hem of his coat,
his infant wail blessing
their harvest.

The Bubäk and the alliance
of nightmare nemeses are valued
Pied Pipers for parents of
the precocious
and self-indulged.

But their price is high,
and their currency is not
monetary.

Or refundable.

Doppelgängers

Doppelgängers are people who have identical appearances, yet no biological connections. It is believed that encountering one's 'twin stranger' is a harbinger of misfortune or potential death. Some believe that these familiar unfamiliars are, in fact, evil twins seeking harm to those they resemble. For hundreds of years, the idea of double spirits or alter egos has remained a popular theme in folklore, mythos, and literature. There are also accounts throughout time from people who have claimed to see their double, only to befall a tragedy following those chance encounters. Such stories bolstered the idea that these physical anomalies were really a nefarious supernatural phenomenon.

The chances of anyone having a bonafide identical lookalike are less than one in a trillion, scientifically. All the same, there have been the rare cases of individuals who have found near identical twins of no relation, and often, these strangers share more than just physical similarities. The notion of that possibility is so bizarre that it lends itself a rich presence in the darkest corners of our imaginations.

Beyond the Looking Glass

That girl in the mirror
smiles in tandem,
bears teeth, opens wide–
I control her.
She is locked in the glass,
looking for me,
      and she knows what to wear
      and how to style my hair
      and how to laugh my laugh–
Silently.

She is anticipated and
reassuring…
She,
the details of my shadow.

I leave her at home
when I emerge
street side –
Safely tucked away
in the vanity mirror upstairs,
only to join me briefly
in the transparent glare of
shop windows passed by.

Her clothes and hair a
wavy implication,
      A watercolour shadow.

I press my palm to hers

and ponder–
Would I welcome her if
she broke free from her prison
and followed?

While I stare at the window
and question my reflection,
I see next to me…
I am doing the same.

Palming her window self,
smiling without my permission,
not a reflection–
        A replication.

        A hiccup.
        A scratch in the vinyl.
        Me on repeat.

She's not my vanity self.
She is wearing my clothes
and my hair
and she is laughing my laugh
Loudly.

Backing away,
she is following me–
That laugh that is mine
        in a different throat
        with my voice.

My mirror self is
a lot less anticipated
and not at all
reassuring

as she walks me off the curb

I barely heard the blare
of the truck horn
    over my laugh.

The Umbra

The backwards hour
brought her to her shadow,
eyes black and h o l l o w,
skin g r e e n and veil thin.
Not a warning, but a promise
that she was spiralling toward
the untimely end of her forever.
A finite farewell to be feared
and spun into dire stories
of what not to do when
wandering the dunes

after dark.

When We See

This dimensional fish tank
we swim through
is the encapsulated
embrace of
uniquity.
We are the one and only,
The original of origins
Unable to see
past our
realm of possibilities.
Safety in confinement.
Safety in the unaware.
Safety until the glass cracks,
and the other side
seeps t h r o u g h.
We are not meant to know
how it is to look upon ourselves–
The moment of meeting our own eyes
and seeing what is, *or isn't,* in their depths;
That moment when we know
the evil within,
the us outside,
is the evil that chases us through
the nightmares we wave away come dawn...
We are immortally our own
worst enemies
and the
keepers of our
own distinctive hells.

We *will* be the d e a t h of we.

Each-uisge

Water horses gallop through a variety of folklore. From the Germanic *Bäckahäst,* to the Welsh *Ceffyl Dŵr* and the Scottish *kelpies*, numerous tales can be found of these beautiful but mischievous water sprites.

While the impish kelpie can be found playing in the rivers and streams throughout Scotland and Great Britain, the vicious *each-uisge* are the water horses of the seas and lochs. These horses can shapeshift into beautiful stallions (or sometimes, handsome men) while on land. Once mounted, they can be hardy farm creatures, so long as they cannot see or smell the water. If it does, the rider on the back of an each-uisge will meet a horrific doom, for its skin turns to glue, trapping the rider on its back. It will return to the water and dive into its depths, drowning the unfortunate rider before devouring them. All that is left of the victim is the liver, which floats to the surface.

It is believed that either shackling an each-uisge around its neck or stealing its magic bridle will prevent the monster from killing its owner. They are also repelled by religious artifacts, like many other demonic entities. Folks are warned to steer away from lone black horses found at the water's edge, as well as anyone seen with seaweed tangled in their hair, lest they really be bloodthirsty sea stallions in disguise.

Liver River

Pony parade,
An equine collective,
The kelpie procession,
Is lining my shore.
A gelding brigade,
Searching for hapless riders,
They're breaching embankments,
They're crossing the moor.

And what I saw coming,
All black silk and seafoam,
Such beautiful creatures,
Such stunning deceit.
The threats I heard humming,
In the calls of such whinnies,
Hid amply the danger,
For those they'd defeat.

I sent out this warning,
To all who would listen,
To avoid those ponies,
That glow in the sun.
For when, by ignoring,
They mounted such stallions,
The horses they captured,
Would begin to run.

And no one will save them,
those foolhardy captives,
Glued to the backsides,

Of river-bound fiends.
They will drown in the waters,
Of the cursed Liver River,
Where only said organ,
Returns to be gleaned.

The Waters of Loch Treig

Local legends said
The farmer's daughter was
No fragile creature,
Stronger than most men.
~ And yet
lithe and lilting and comely.

Tending the livestock
And harvesting the fields,
Fair voice rising
To bless the breezes.
~ She longed
for her own valiant mate.

One Spring afternoon
She encountered the stranger,
A man solitary
Lingering by the loch.
~ His hair
a tangle of wet seaweed.

A stunning lad
Though she ran, nonetheless.
She recalled warnings
About strangers beside water.
~ Even though
her heart found him alluring.

Moons passed by
Until one Autumn afternoon

A black stallion
Appeared in the fields.
~ His coat
shimmered green in the sunset.

Such a spirited creature!
So she graced his neck
With a silver shackle
To tame the steed.
~ Christened *Treig*
for her ancestral home's loch.

The farmer envied
His daughter's shimmering horse
And pressed often
To control the reins.
~ Always refused
with her most gentle smile.

Until ill fortune
Struck the farmer's mare lame
As he prepared
To market their crops.
~ She relinquished
Treig's reins to her father.

After they disappeared
Over the hill's rise
The silver shackle
Appeared at her feet.
~ Her wails
were lost to the wind.

Toward Loch Treig
The horse carried him,

Black coat slick
With an inexorable glue.
~ His screams
silenced in cold, dark waters.

The daughter searched
But found neither him
Nor the steed
Along the loch's shores.
~ Vowing never
to leave them, she remained.

Counting the tides
And cursing the moon
Her cries answered as
Her father's liver floated by.

~ Eternity's warning
to avoid riding strange horses.

Hellhounds

If dogs are man's best friend, then *hellhounds* are Death's best friend. These underworldly puppos are plentiful in both literature and mythology, with many renowned enough as to be recognized by their individual names. From Cerebus, Hades' guard to the gates of the Underworld, to the Yeth Hound, a headless dog of Devon folklore, hellhounds are *almost* as beloved as their living counterparts.

Of course, hellhounds are a bit less affectionate than mankind's canine companions. They are typically described as oversized, covered in black, mangy fur, with eyes that glow red from fire. They also bear a distinctly foul odor. Some have growls that are heard across miles of countryside, even when the beasts aren't visible, while others are accompanied by the sounds of rattling chains. They are often considered guardians of old churches and graveyards, and, occasionally seen as benign and even helpful. They are known as portents of misfortune and approaching storms.

But the legend most frequently attached to hellhounds is the curse they carry when one stares into their eyes. It is told that anyone who looks into the eyes of a hellhound three times will soon perish. Any traveler on the roads at night will do well to avoid stumbling across these hair-raising harbingers of death.

Bringer

Were you once the shadow
on the grounds of the rectory,
Solitary *Church Grym*...
Pacing the steps of a chapel
Neither hell, nor holy,
The rumble of your growl
enough to chill souls.

Or maybe you were the wanderer
that emerged from the darkness
of passages outside the castle...
Westward guardian haunting
the Isle of Man –
Reaper of the reckless
Elusive *Moddey Ghoo*.

Tonight, I fear you are
the vicious *Barghest* beast,
lurking in the Snickelways
of a northern Yorkshire city,
waiting for me with
Fire-filled eyes and
the rattle of chains...

Your deadliest claw bearing
my dispatch to Hell.

The Whist Hound

Across the moors
The ash curtain of dusk darkens
To a starless sky with a pale sentinel moon
As a beast prowls the edge on this coldest of nights
Disturbing the frigid highland with growls
That quiver woody heathers

...

Red flames where his eyes should be
Howls that echo across stones and through reeds
It is not Cerberus wandering the
Road to Dartmoor

...

But the solitary spectre seeking his path
Cabell's charge ravages the grounds of Buckfast Abbey
Looming in the ruins of a hellish blaze
Pacing the sepulchre
By night

...

Binding the devil's unholy pact.

Three Strikes

I found my path homeward
under a Fool September Moon,
streets bathed in silver and granite,
the smell of bonfire in my nostrils as
I searched for smoke in the dark
only to find the murky shadows
of houses, streetlamps, and trees.
I almost didn't see what I could feel
watching me in the evening gloom,
a canine shadow lurking behind...
Tracing my footsteps,
    The scent of ash in its fur.

A round of drinks with friends
at a pub tucked deep in Dublin,
our loud songs invading the sky
as we swagger a maze of alleys.
Each of us takes our leave
at our own proper doorways
until I remained alone–the weary
wanderer seeking safe refuge.
Yes, I knew it was watching,
the smell of flame just beyond...
Growls shiver the air,
    fangs shine through dark.

A fortnight has placed me on
the back roads of a small town.
It has taken two seasons to retrace
the avenues of childhood folly.

Another Fool Moon highlights the
graceful rise of farm pastures and
valleys, the lone silhouette of
the black beast stalking my journey.
As the smoke fills my head, I know
the next time our paths cross will
not be under the moon…
   But on the road to *Hell*.

Jinn

Jinn (also known as *Djinn* or the Anglicized *Genie*) are supernatural beings rooted in both pre-Islamic Arabian and Islamic theology and mythos. These enigmatic creatures straddle a blurry line between their roots in ancient religions and modern mythologies. While sometimes grouped with demons and devils, jinn actually fall between humans and divinities, and as such, are not automatically evil or good, as they are created with free will to determine this for themselves. They are not immortal, and they experience the same needs and desires as humans, but despite their similarities, jinn are not usually visible to human eyes.

Often, jinn are portrayed as beautiful women who appear to tempt men, but who are indistinguishable from human women, save for the donkey's hooves they walk on instead of feet. They sometimes hide in natural objects, such as rocks, or in desert sand, or inside windstorms, and can shapeshift into various animals. They have been associated with disease and disaster and have been accused of demonic possession.

Perhaps the most popular version that appears in literature is the genie, trapped in an oil lamp, waiting to be of service to the fortunate master who stumbles across their prison. However, that benevolent wish-granting spirit of books and television is actually an *afarit*–a malevolent demon that may be called forth for its assistance. Rather than rubbing random bottles, one would lay a *tasksut* (a steam pot used for cooking couscous) over an oil lamp. When an invocation is recited, the many heads of the afarit appear in the holes of the pot, ready to be commanded. If one is calm and confident, the afarit will comply. But these demons can possess humans and will readily do so, should they choose to turn on their summoner.

Afarits can also slip into our world on their own. When someone is murdered, the spilled blood creates a portal that the demon can pass through. The only way to intercept it is to drive a previously unused nail through the puddle of blood. Removing that nail will free the afarit.

By Blood

Afarit appears
in a puddle
of blood,
no nail
waits
there
that
will
be
his
bar.
Called
by the evil
of a murderer's
rage, a demon ready
to rain his agony on the
souls of mortals, summoned
through pain and brutality,
this Jinn will punish
without favor.
A merciless
demon in
the belly of
a bottle, you use a
tasksut to lure him out
and *maybe*, if so disposed,
he will grant your desire. But be
watchful, be wary... if you act hastily,
he may well tear you asunder, limb by limb.
This malicious creature – this contemptuous cur
is a monster that blackens the heart of men who call
his name. Beware of blood puddles, beware of gold
bottles; fight the desire of greed within a genie's gift.
Because the price asked is higher than a gemstone's
worth when it's the value of your blood in portal
puddles and an Asfarit's opened doorway.
Nothing comes so freely, ever.
Keep a nail in your
pocket,
and keep your
hands off occupied bottles.

Jinni

Whirling dervish of Midnight's sun,
the itinerant furyfunnel
craving the decay of rotting corpses,
    she searches…
Shimmering lady of the windstorm –
The beast upon the desert.

Siren of the sand
calls them from the horizon,
waits in the rocks at their feet –
    She hungers…
The same creature of fire
that lures them across dunes.

A mirage of malevolence
hovering everywhere and nowhere –
Every soul that desires,
    She devours…
Satiated only by blood and flesh –
The beast upon the desert.

Niyan Theory

Dark cadmium,
shifting sands sculpting
new landscapes along
the southern route
of the ancient Silk Road,

where towns of refuge
bowed their heads
to the fury of desert winds.

They were adapted –
Acclimated to life skirting
the Taklamakan,

when the lure of riches carried
merchants 5000 miles
to the Levantine Sea.

Tangible monsters
were the faces of thieves
and the devil of starvation,
but what remained unseen –
    the face inside
    the sandstorm,
    the fury of the dunes…

She, the *al-ghaib*
swept the roads bare
and buried Niya
under a century of scorn.

Leaving only ruins
of an ancient oasis
    in the Sea of Death.

Melon Heads

Among newer urban legends are stories of the *melon heads*. These beings, as the name implies, have bulbous heads, and have been spotted in specific towns in the states of Michigan, Connecticut, and Ohio. It is claimed they hide in the woods along certain roads and attack people who come close.

Despite the geographical differences, legends of the melon heads remain basically the same and have other notable similarities. In each state, the melon heads were once patients in a nearby hospital, children who suffered from a disfiguring condition called Hydrocephalus, a disease which resulted in having large heads due to cerebral fluid accumulating on their brains. There was a doctor (even bearing the same last name of Crowe in two of the stories) who performed cruel experiments on them that further exacerbated their condition. The melon heads later attacked and killed the doctor, shortly before the hospital caught fire. In some accounts, they ate the doctor, in others, they chopped him up and scattered him around the hospital. They then escaped into the surrounding woods, where they remain to this day.

The stories about the hospitals have never been substantiated, regardless of the location, and there is no record of a Doctor Crowe. There are sometimes buildings nearby that are reputed to be the old hospital, but there are no records that show such buildings were ever the hospitals named in the reports. Additionally, these legends always involve a dark, heavily wooded road nicknamed Dracula Drive. There are usually corresponding tales of crybaby bridges reported in those areas, too, that are believed to be connected with the melon heads. These are bridges one can park on at midnight and hear the sounds of a baby crying from the river below.

In Connecticut, there are a number of other legends that revolve around people suffering from mutations or deformities…proof that people are easily frightened by human conditions they simply don't understand.

Chardon Township, Crying

The winding snake Wisner
slithers over Crybaby Bridge.
Under this blanket of skydark,
lost cries swim the river.

Curtains of trees, shadow eyes
of the children, wait
just beyond the road.

Did that voracious brood feast on *crow*
before they burned in their beds, their
cold caskets set ablaze…
the mangled and bloated creatures
mutated and too head-heavy to escape?

Charred carcasses escape to
a sanctuary of barren woodlands
that hugs a twisting spine river…
not far from their ruins of torture –

not far from where the innocent
became the flesh-devourers,
freeing infant screams to the moon.

Never stop on that bridge
to search darkened shoulders,
lest the Hungry are waiting
beneath the rusted steel
that carries Wisner over its
deluge of souls.

Dracula Drive

Black
Serpentine curves
Slice through bare trees,
Snow shoulders, and
Pothole ice
Miles
Away from
Safe warm beds.
They wait out there...
Beyond the cast
Of headlights:
Hungry,
Predacious,
a twisted menace.
The barely human
Monstrosities
Stalk
Blood in the air.
They wait for you...
Lurking beyond
A dead-end
Abyss.

New Animals

Land of wolverines
    and *wobbleheads*.
    The woods beside
    the great lake shiver
above their sanctum.

In the caverns of an
    abandoned zoo
    are new animals
with swollen skulls
and water brains–

Once…they were children.

Once…they were humans.

Now they scavenge
and ravage and attack
anyone coming close
    enough to pose danger.
    Their home, an asylum,
    before it was a prison,
faded into murmurs of myth.

The body of their keeper–
massacred and dismembered,
chopped into pieces was
sprinkled like salt around
the rooms of the sanatorium.

Hell seasoned with blood
    and with pain
transmuted the innocent
into modern monstrosities.

    Such
    devastating degradations–

they hide in the caves
    beneath
Robinson Township–

New animals hunt those woods.

Mermaids

Who doesn't love a good *mermaid*? A beloved favorite of popular family films and cartoons, these magical half-fish, half-humans are a nearly universally recognized character. Mermaids have appeared in fairy tales and mythology and are most often depicted as kind and helpful creatures, and the offspring of King Neptune. They are gifted with characteristics and superpowers that can bring redemption to humanity.

Ironically, the early depictions of mermaids were not so charming. Thousands of years ago, Greek mythology included stories of beings known as *sirens*, women who were part fish with bird beaks and who sang to the sailors at sea in order to lure them into treacherous waters or against rocks. In time, descriptions of these creatures changed into what are now known as mermaids. Their objectives were the same, however. Seamen believed that mermaids sat on rocks in the ocean and attempted to lure them to their deaths through their great beauty and angelic voices.

Today, popular cosplay trends include *Mermaiding*, an activity in which a woman (or a man) wears a costume mermaid tail...sometimes for the purpose of swimming, and sometimes for choreographed performances similar to water ballet. Others simply wear them for photographic opportunities. For a creature that started with such nefarious intentions, mermaids have metamorphosed completely into the darlings of fashionable fantasy.

Chum

She offered her jewel for your love,
a voice so precious, it was traded
for a moment of your adoration,
a lifetime of your consistency.

Her voice stirred the waves
between her home and your shore,
it was the crystalline echo in your head
that first lured you to the waters.

But now that she walks silent for you,
the photophores in her eyes are dulled
and her aquatic grace is clumsy, dried.
You change your mind and direction
and you cast her fate to the tidal wave
        she is ill-equipped to tread.

You forget about the sacrifice
the sea made for your pleasure,

return to the sea as a man of the world,
a king on a vessel you didn't deserve.
The sea doesn't forgive your disregard
and it tears your hull open upon its rocks.

You forgot the place she called home, so
she returns to the surface to find clinging
and pleading for that moment of mercy–
a moment of grace you once denied her

when her voice was gone and her legs
were gaunt.

The glow in her eyes isn't adoration
and the twist of her smile doesn't know love.
But villiform teeth you don't recognize
are the consequence of your audacity,
and they will tear your flesh quicker than
you tore her heart.

Daughter of

Daughter of
Daughter of Atargatis
carries her mother's pain
in her veins –
waits beneath the crest of each wave
and hides in the ocean current,
crushing and capsizing,
    destruction
in a pretty package,

her lilting voice
    a requiem.

They die with a smile.

Slithering
through the wreckage,
through the busted holes
in sea-rotted wood,
death treasures wait,
    twisted
in her brackish locks.

Pirate bone ornaments and
gold coins
rendered useless rest
miles below their last sunsets,

miles below where
    she sang.

They died with a smile.

Daughter of
Daughter of Atargatis.

Siren Seduction

Come closer...
I call you
From a distant bank,
A mirage among waves of
Cerulean and Bimini waters

My voice, the twill
Of a sea sparrow,
An enticing lilt
That embraces your soul
And pulls you near...

Blinded by spray
But guided by timbre

I sing to you
A paradise melody
Of soft beaches,
Softer skin,
An ecstasy so indescribable
It can only be seen
Through your pulse

You steer your vessel
In the direction
Of soft leeward breezes,
Seaweed tangling my hair
Sand robing my flesh
Inviting you in

My song, this scintillating prophecy
luring you as facilely
As a fish on a line

And you may not understand
How I remain
As tantalizing as I am:
Elusive
Unattainable...
Incomprehensible

You will understand
When your bow shatters
Upon the sharp edges
Of an angry reef
And your body tears open
On coral the color of my lips

You accepted my invitation...

Seafaring supplicant
Submerged submissive.

You sink into my depths.

Mothmen

The legend of the *Mothman* started in northern West Virginia in November of 1966, when five men working in a cemetery witnessed an unidentifiable creature flying low above the trees near the town of Clendenin. A few days later, two couples claimed to see this same creature as they were making a night drive past an area that used to house a WWII munitions plant. After that, sightings of the mysterious creature were reported across Point Pleasant, a town situated by the Ohio River. All of the accounts matched. It was described as a man between six to seven feet tall, with enormous wings spanning around 10 feet, and two large, round eyes that glowed red in the dark. Without conclusive photographic evidence, researchers proposed the sightings were of various birds that people mistook for the creepy cryptid, such as barred owls or sandhill cranes.

A year later, December 1967, the Silver Bridge collapsed, sending 46 people to their deaths in the icy river. Townsfolk connected the Mothman appearances to the tragedy. Some speculated the Mothman tampered with the bridge and caused the structural failure, but others believed the Mothman's presence was meant to warn them of the impending disaster. From then on, the creature has been described as a harbinger that signals coming doom.

Claims of appearances from around the world associate the Mothman with tragedies, such as in Russia before the 1999 apartment bombings, and as recently as Chicago in 2017, when 55 reports of sightings were made. Every fall, a Mothman Festival is held in Point Pleasant, and tens of thousands from all over travel to celebrate the town's most notorious visitor.

Bicentennial Bridge

November
on the river is
haunted by wing shadows
crossing graveyards and bridges
red-eyed glares and word-
less warnings.
November
nineteen sixty-
six, small town hysteria is
no more than munitions mayhem
or Lovers Lane pranksters.
Come December
the Ohio
will be filled with
bodies and presents and
cars–and the souls of forty–six
who drowned in the icy
river below the
Silver span.
Were they victims
of malfunction, or were
they victims of wicked destruction,
bloated and frozen and
forever attached to
a harbinger?
In November twenty-
sixteen, the elusive shadow
returned to the skies above the river,
a portentous homecoming.
Does a new nightmare
wait in the Ohio
b e l o w?

Could Have Been

In the days before East End caught fire,
the beast hovered over the streets–
a shadow perched on rooftops,
a black bastion against
yellow streetlights
...Could have been an owl.

Round eyes burned red pain
through anyone whose path it crossed.
Some deaf, some blind…
All tormented by revelation,
hysterical and unrecognizable
...Could have been a heron.

Signalling the rampant blaze
that devoured every home
and choked the townsfolk with
the noxious fumes of earthly hell,
East End left a smouldering labyrinth
at the end of Highway 47.

If only they knew then what
they would know soon enough –
Danger lies behind what is seen.

...*Could* have been a sand crane.

But it wasn't.

Dead Zone

Do you suppose
in the days before the inferno,
the people of Pripyat
entertained an enigmatic guest?
    Do you?

Did anyone see
it circling the skyline,
and wonder at the span
of its terrible wings?

Did the children
hurl stones
    at an ugly bird?
Would their parents
notice when they did?

Did that spectral shadow with
round reflector eyes
and wings the size
of tattered sails,

perch in the commons,
hover above playgrounds,
swoop over cars?

Could they feel the
sinister presence

resting on the bridge

where they would later watch
    Chernobyl burn,
    oblivious bodies,
    under the soft fall
    of radiated ash
and certain doom?

Vampires

Vampires. Those sexy, smoldering blood-sucking lotharios with the dark brooding eyes and glorious hair and a menacing but alluring sarcasm. Yes, vampires are the rockstars of monsters. The icing on the horror cake. There are countless books and films that twist Vampire lore into steamy paranormal romances, and they all have a broad and adoring audience, so much so, that vampires are often the heroes in these stories, and their slayer, the villains.

But what we know as that charming, bitey seducer looked and behaved differently before the early 19th century. Vampires were monsters in the truest sense, dating back a millennium. Early vampires were darker, the color of rot, their bodies bloated and oozing blood out of their facial orifices. Their hair and nails would grow long, but not so much the teeth. This was believed to be an exemplification of what society knew of death, rather than evidence of a supernatural being. Plus in these stories, anyone could become a vampire, not just those who were bitten. A lot of superstitions circled around these undead terrors, and it was simple things like an animal jumping across a dead body that could cause a person to return to the land of the living as a bloodthirsty beast.

Staking is the most popular method for slaying a vampire, but depending on the culture, it wasn't always the heart that was targeted. Some cultures believed in staking them through the mouth or stomach. Others believed they must be decapitated to truly kill them. Suspected vampires were buried with pieces of steel embedded throughout their bodies. Sometimes items such as bricks, lemons, or garlic cloves were shoved in their mouth before burial as a means of protection. Sometimes boiling water or Holy Water was poured over the remains. Cremation of the body and the coffin was another method to prevent a vampire's return from the grave.

Vampires in literature showed up by the 17th century, but while it was far from the first of its kind, Bram Stoker's *Dracula* became the roots for a new genre of fiction centered around these creatures of the night.

Bat Evolution

I was a bat in my last life,
Dizzy on sound and sunset,
Congregating in the dark lush of caves.

Erratic avoidance was not just customary–
It was approved,
And I wore it as an eager cloak,

Dancing in circles across orange skies,
Sonar synced and synchronized,
Deliberately delirious.

In the height of such spectacle,
My teeth found soft meat
Soaked in copper and sinew.

I was no longer a bat,
But a fiend starved for blood,
Preying from the shadows of alleys,

Searching the streets for pale throats,
Frenetic pulses above lace collars–
Felled victims of my thrall.

Each kiss of sustenance was a tonic,
A potion of transformation,
A reflection I see only in eyes widened in fear.

Long legs, long fingers, longer fangs–
I once was a bat a century past,

But eternal life demands a body count–
So now I am a monster.

Exsanguination

Fangs glow in the moonlight
  Like polished ivory.
  Or bleached bone.
Sharp jewels ready to draw
ruby and garnet rhinestones from
the pale vellum of flesh
  with pierce precision.

A decadent fiend with a hunger
  for fulfilled fantasies,
preys on the vulnerable,
  the sleeping.
Their blood, pliant bedcap beckoning
  from bedroom corners
  and hallway passages,
pricks the senses of this senseless beast.

It calls them from the depths of dreams.

Should they wake from consumption with
battered soul intact? They will not evoke
  the sensation of cold steel penetrating their veins
  or the jagged tear of nails across their pulse
  or the urgent whisper rush of life dwindling
  between the teeth of their vanquisher.

They will only recall the fall
of rubies and garnets
  and ivory
falling across the shiver of
  paper-pale
  flesh.

Thrall

She sinks into my flesh,
this dagger-toothed
    adrenaline,
This glorious creature
breaching my window.

Her hands stroke glaciers
down the column of my throat
and I feel no
    warmth
in her tongue's caress.

Velvet whispers in my ear
sing of heaven and rapture,
but I know this slow
    seduction
is an admission to hell.
I don't understand my
invitation to her touch –

    My heart yields to men.
    My fingers bear mortal bonds.

Still, I lay opened, eager
for this darkly intrusion –
I, her most willing captive
of blood-soaked
    desire.

Wendigoag

The *wendigo* (*wendigoag* in its plural form) is an evil creature that feasts on human flesh. It comes from the traditional folklore of the First Nation Algonquian Tribes who lived in the north, from Nova Scotia to the eastern coast of Canada and around the Great Lakes region. Tales of it were told as a warning against greed, taboo behaviors, and cannibalism. They believed anyone consuming human flesh, whether because of greed, or sheer survival, would be possessed by the spirit of the wendigo and transformed into a monstrous beast.

Wendigoag vaguely resembles humans, though they are severely emaciated with gray skin, yellow elongated teeth, and claws. Often, they do not have lips because they have chewed them off. They grow larger in proportion to the size of whatever human they devour, and therefore, they are always starving. This causes them to grow to giant sizes, and their hunger is never satiated, no matter how much they eat. In Western pop culture, the wendigo tends to be described as a furry creature with large antlers or horns, but such details do not fit the authentic depictions of the Algonquian folklore.

The Cree of the Great Lakes region holds a ceremonial dance to warn against the dangers of excessive greed and cannibalism as a way to reinforce its taboo among younger generations. There is also a condition that doctors call wendigo psychosis where a patient craves human flesh and fears becoming a cannibal. This is a culture-bound syndrome, meaning it is only prevalent in modern indigenous communities.

Iron Woman

North of the northern lake,
the Iron Woman waits.

> She knows I'll come.
She has seen me prowling
Through her pipe-smoke visions,
in the line of the horizon,
> Out of the meat of forest.

I was young, too young…
when the tribal elders danced
the wiindigookaanzhimowin
backwards around drums
to warn of the hunger
> that infects a soul and
> putrefies starved flesh.

I forgot the stories that
swam in my blood,
as I stumbled in search of
victuals, finding my
single salvation in a
> chance cadaver

bloated and buried
and anointed with
fresh fallen snow.

The inexplicable ache of hunger

twisting my body became my pulse
as I scavenged the woodlands.

I found myself the pursued,
Distant guns aimed at my back
Fired by men I could break in one hand
　　–if I only desire.

They don't know I am preternatural.
They don't know I am trapped inside,
a prison of bone and monstrosity,
a victim of the tantalizing taste of
tissues and sinew tangled between
my teeth.

My appetite consumes me
faster than I consume others.

Now other stories come,
stories foggy and imprecise…
Tales of the *Two Spirit*, a shaman
who could eat curses and banish the
evil seeds sown.

The Iron Woman of the northern lake.

She has sent me the invitation–
a summons from far beyond far.
Either find myself in her,
　　or find my death on her blade.

If she can lend me a *Manitou*
　　for my final quest
I will gladly fall on that knife.

Because
redemption is not found in shotgun casings
      and thirst is never sated with stolen blood.

Lusus Naturae (Indigenous Curse)

It lies beyond the yard
past the trees that cloak horizon,
roams in silvered darkness with
sharp eyes and sharper teeth.

Familiar and foreign and furious,
Its veins full of something colder
than a January night
and emptier than a chasm.

It came first in a dream,
hungry and feral, a shredding fugue
lurking in memories at sunrise–
a promise for the new nightfall.

It remembers the path it took
crossing miles by moonlight's grace,
up to the door of the midnight house–
the known and unknown nightmare.

No Cure for Cannibal

The taste for flesh
Lengthens the teeth
Strengthens the eyes
and the hunger.
    Quickens the pulse
    Of the *Ever* Now *Never*
Sharpens the nose
to slight traces of copper.

Hunched behind trees
and running the back roads
Shrouded in darkness
as cold as Winter's ire.
Tracking a feast of
Warm blood and soft meat
and the naivety of
souls that won't believe.

Sin and sinew never satiate
Pits of curse and empty
Growing into bottomless chasms
Seeking elusive relief.

Ever Now *Never*

Hunger feeds evil,
    Feeds
What *used* to be
    Warm.

Werewolves

Werewolves are humans that shapeshift into wolves under the full moon. In wolf form, they hunt for food, which is usually other humans or animals, and then feed until sunrise. It is believed that a bite or scratch from a werewolf can infect others with the condition. It is also alleged that one can become a werewolf by being cursed. Often, the unfortunate human afflicted with the condition will be unaware that they are a werewolf, as they experience blackouts and lost time when they shift into their bestial form.

Stories of werewolves can be found in literature as far back as ancient Greek Mythology with tales of the Neuri tribe, and King Lycaon of Arcadia. Germanic and Scandinavian lore were also frequented with legends of these creatures. Their presence throughout all of Europe was feared, and reports of vicious werewolf attacks were commonly recorded. Werewolvery was a charge often attached to accused witches, most notably in the Vaud and Valais witch trials of the early 15th century, and this accusation persisted in similar cases through Europe well into the 18th century.

Older traditions of curing the werewolf condition included exorcisms, surgeries, or medicinally with herbs like wolfsbane. It was believed that striking the wolf on the head with a scalpel or driving a nail through its claws could also remove the affliction. The introduction of silver bullets occurred later, particularly in the 19th century, and remains the most popular method for felling the beast.

Arcadian Dynasty

On the summit of
Mount Lycaon,
Near the place where
no shadows fall,
The ash-heap altar remains
where they were born–
This ancient feral bloodline.

Sons of sons of ephebes,
Gathered initiates devouring
slain flesh to exalt
their *Lycaean Zeus*–
All obedient carnivores
and one oblivious cannibal,
Tinged by a forbidden pact.

For *he* who partakes of man
becomes monster apostate–
Wolf Zeus eats the body of the boy.
Nine years trapped in beast skin,
Roaming the mountain in hunger.
Bellies growl for mortal meat,
The taste of blood in their teeth.

It is said when Darmarchus turned
he endured his curse refusing consumption–
A tribute to intention and integrity,
His disease revoked–his flesh restored.

But…

How many more failed and feasted?
Their lives and lines condemned
to be forever wolves hunting under
the Arcadian moon.

La Bête

Prints in the mud
Cupping
small puddles of curse.
Those who drink
forget everything but
Jeziah's appetite–
the beast's contract
infects the thirsting soul
Shoves memory into
the black of nothing
as people lose
their throats–
their heads–
their lives.

The headless corpses of villagers
litter the hillsides of the Margerides.

Jeziah withered on his
sister's arrow
of mistletoe and ash,
but his spirit is a bloodline
rekindling.
Every
blood moon brings
    A new bite
    A new spawn
    A new chapter

For *La Bête du Gevaudan.*

Pheremonious

Your beast calls to mine
under the red halo of a full harvest moon,
Feral and sanctimonious
Tethered to hunger and desire
And the abandonment of satiation.
I hear you as the thudding pulse,
The frenetic and insatiable urge
to sink our fangs into soft flesh feasting
All copper wine and meat tartar.
We take our fill from the unwitting
and congregate in celebration,
Seeking a deeper drink of pleasure
to ease the pains of our transitions.
Bound and *pheremonious...*
Mortal and monster and cursed.

The streets are warm and safe by day,
Its nightmares tucked away tightly
by a therapist's couch and useless prescriptions
I will never see filled.
I pass the thin, tall stranger on the sidewalk
and turn to see eyes lock mine,
Red and haunted and hungry
Remembering midnight's depravity.
I don't know him, but my blood does,
Bound and *pheremonious...*
Waiting for me and the next full moon.

Will-o'-the-wisps

Will-o'-the-wisps are mysterious and ghostly lights that appear at night along roads, over wetlands, in graveyards, and many other places all over the world. Sometimes they are seen as balls of light; sometimes, they appear as a flickering flame. Fool's fire, ghost candles, spook lights, orbs, hinkypunk, and jack-o-lanterns are but a handful of the names that have been used to describe this eerie phenomenon.

Many cultures believe these lights are spirits of the dead, or mischievous fairies, that appear to lead people into dangerous places. Others believe they are demons. They are often described in folktales as candles or lanterns carried by characters named Will or Jack, who have been doomed to wander in the dark as punishment for their bad behavior. Commonly, they are believed to be markers where treasures are buried. In Brazil, the lights are associated with a large demon snake that eats the eyes of animals and corpses. In places such as Trinidad, and even the state of Louisiana, these lights are associated with evil spirits that seek to suck the blood from their victims.

Of course, these legends are so pervasive because will-o'-the-wisp are the product of an unextraordinary reaction known as bioluminescence, a result of gasses that are created from organic decay common to wet areas. But to the unsuspecting traveler of earlier centuries, a sudden flickering ball of light dancing in front of them could easily be mistaken for a devious devil seeking to drown them in the rush of dark rivers or lose them forever to a dangerous swamp.

Along the Spooklight Highway

Ball of fire
dancing the devil's promenade,
spinning in the dirt…
tripping across borders
in the Ozark dark.

The fire trails the passage

where the Quapaw lovers
took their lives
in the depths of Spring River;

and
where the Osage chief
combs the way for his
guillotined head;

and
where the widowed miner
searches for his missing
wife and children.

Does ignis fatuus
hover by the tear-
scarred trail over
a century behind?

The haunted beauty of
bioluminescent decay…

Somewhere outside
    of Joplin,
the Spooklights travel
Star Route South 43

Under Missourian sky.

Chasing Fireflies

Dusk in the damplands
leaves orange trails across
gray waters,
Everything green
caked in mud brown

Brackish lagoons showcase
the pollen and dust
that hugs everything
the eye touches.

As the sun ducks behind trees,
The dark of the swamp
is punctuated with a pulse

A flicker of energy
A spark that shivers
as it rises from mire

this floating orb of light
dancing between trees and
cypress knees.
The glow beckons

promises of warmth,
Of childhood laughter
and twilight magic.

A firefly spirit
begging for chase.

Don't go.

It knows its direction;
It meanders with intention;
It leads into the thick...

And leaves you there.

Fool's Fire

The rise of the road
through the distant black night
is propped against a
    cobalt sky
And paint-spattered flints
of flickering white.

I've been out here for days,
chasing the distance,
enticed by a fireball
that hovers ahead:

Always out of reach,
bouncing and shifting,
Exploding and shrinking,
 whispering...

No one hears the call,
But me.

The distant chant.
That leering grab.

The need to hold the fire
    in my palm
and feel something warm...
    Anything.

    Finally. Fully.
My stilled lungs filled with sludge,

my soul forever
chasing flames
      t h r o u g h the woods.

Disappearing in the bog.

Always
reaching for the light.

Wraiths

Wraith is the Scottish word for a ghost, though they are far more than simple spirits. Usually, they are the revenant of a wizard or sorcerer who used black magic in their lifetime to bend time or grant themselves immortality. They become immortal but are cursed to wander between the dimensions of the living and the dead without any possibility of finding their afterlife. As a result, they are full of extreme emotions like rage and hatred.

Some can steal the souls of humans, and unless that wraith is killed, those souls will belong to the wraith eternally. Others are parasitic and seek to possess the souls of innocent humans. In such instances, should a human possessed by a wraith bear a child, the wraith attaches to them, as well, creating a *blood child*. Only one kind of wraith, known as a *vorer*, is considered harmless. These wraiths attach to individuals for the entirety of their lives, and simply shadow them without ever causing them harm.

Wraiths do not bear any substantial marked physical traits. They are typically described, if at all, as a dark figure in a black cloak. They are usually just an evil presence that can be felt, rather than seen. They suck humans dry of the emotions that keep them vital and lively, and that is how one can tell when they are in the presence of such a malignant demon–by the sudden, unexplainable feelings of hopelessness and fury.

Damnatorum

To walk in the in between
the real and the not
vessel of fury and pain,
Revenant.

A prisoner of Purgatory
vindictive, the vague shadow
seeking the unsuspecting mortal
Rapacious.

Eternally bound and
born of banishment
the exiled immortal
Rancorous.

Vengeful wisp
wicked wanderer
soul stealer
Ravenous.

Renounced
Removed
Reviled
Rage.

Infinite Unattained

The stealer of souls waits
between
life and death–
Here and hereafter

Stirring angry in the void,
stalking shadows–

Whispering
threats that sound
like night breezes
and curtain falls.

It's hungry for a peek
behind the veil,
Yet is always refused
    passage into
the only eternity
    worthy of
    their
    perfection.

Their only Heaven

forever
beyond their reach.

Upon My Soul's Departure

I want not to forever roam;

seeking my reflection eternal
but unable to rest or reappear.
Pressed in between time like
a dried rose flattened in
the pages of
a book.

A vagrant wisp without home.

An invisible cardboard flat
poised inside the bars I used
to frequent, or just outside
the churches I
refused to
enter.

My beauty decayed like rot;

The stench of lingering soul
wafting around my revenant,
so they will never see, yet
always know when
I've returned
to collect
them.

Damned to exist only to not.

Collecting unsuspecting souls
as an offering to buy passage
into the Paradise beyond this
Nowhere; endlessly bound
to haunt the nothing as
a wraith outside
the Being.

I will not ask to live forever.

Yokai

Yokai is the term ascribed to anything that falls within supernatural, superstitious, and/or religious parameters of the Japanese people. Traditional oral folklore in Japan dates back as far as the 8th century, but in the early 1600s, a rise in popularity flooded Japanese culture and manifested itself in art and literature. During this time, bestiaries were compiled that defined and detailed the many otherworldly creatures of folklore, and from this, the yokai were introduced to the world. Some yokai were monsters, demons, spirits, ghosts…others were creatures that were mostly human, and others were spirits invested in environmental elements such as weather events and natural disasters. Pretty much everything imaginable was designated by a yokai, even down to the mundane daily tasks such as cooking and housekeeping.

Kekkai are an ugly sort whose name translates to 'blood clot', and they are small monkey-like beasts with backwards hair and double tongues, one white and one red. When a new mother does not receive proper medical treatment during her pregnancy, she will sometimes give birth to this monster instead of a child. Once born, the kekkai attempt to escape between the floorboards, or sometimes by scaling the pothook above the hearth. If they are not stopped, they hide underneath the house and wait until their mothers fall sleep, at which time they burrow back up through the floorboards and tear into her body. Should bamboo screens be placed around the perimeter of the home, they will create a spiritual barrier that will trap the kekkai beneath the house and prevent them from killing their mothers. This yokai was used to explain childbirth tragedies such as birth defects and miscarriages before modern medicine intervened.

Gashadokuro, or "rattling skull," is a ninety-foot skeleton that roams country roads, seeking victims. It produces a rattling noise but will be perfectly silent when it is sneaking up on unsuspecting travelers. If it finds such unfortunate wayfarers, it will either crush them or bite off their heads. The creature is fueled by the anger and despair of hundreds of fallen soldiers and starved travelers who died along the roads and were never buried. These monsters were prevalent in areas near large battlefields because of the many souls that perished there. As wartime dwindled, so did the existence of these fearsome behemoths.

Arachnophobes will find *jorōgumo* particularly terrifying, for while the name translates to "entangling bride," the jorōgumo is a Golden Orb Weaver spider. These spiders are usually a few centimeters in size but can grow large enough to eat small birds and prey. Traditional folktales say these weavers can live for hundreds of years, amassing incredible magical powers. As their power grows, so does their appetites, and they turn to humans for their food. The jorōgumo will transform into a beautiful woman that lures delectable young men into her home by promising them love or favors. She then spins them into a web of unbreakable silk and will feast on them slowly for days at a time, until they eventually die. There is no cure or defense against a jorōgumo, so any unfortunate fellow lured into her den is surely doomed.

The popularity of yokai crashed after the Edo period in the mid-1800s but regained new interest after WWII. Today, Yokai have grown a universal appeal and have been embraced by pop culture, film, cartoons, manga, and anywhere else where horror is celebrated.

Blood Clot (gogyohka)

Through sweat
Through screams
A moment of magic
Manifested
With pain

To her detriment
A legacy born
But the child expected
Loud, pink
Round-eyed

Emerged as creature
Coarse and gray,
Double tongued and
Covered in blood
A hearth-bound fury

Without *Shamoji*
Or gold-leafed *Byobu*
It burrows the ground
Beneath the house
Beneath her bed.

Forgotten abscess
Abomination festering
Dismissed as misfortune
This *Kekkai* nightmare
Waits to reoccur

Sunrise breaks darkness
For everyone except
Mommy-less-Dear
Her body eviscerated
Consumed from below.

Jorōgumo's Song (tanka)

Gossamer shimmer
Hovering in silken threads
She hunts from above
Watching from darkest corners
Spinning her sinister web.

Brought upon her path
A man from another world
Looking for refuge
Requesting a night's shelter
Road weary and exhausted.

She smiled her welcome
As he entered her parlour
Her soft lilting song
Coaxing him from his travels
Offering invitation.

That voice, a caress
Promising him nirvana
Harp strings resonate
Melodious seduction
Symphonious distraction.

Soprano siren
So entranced, he doesn't see
Eight legs emerging...
Hungry enchantress
Ready to feast on his soul.

Road Hazard (haiku)

The night is not safe
for the lonely travelers
of countryside roads.

    When ears start to ring,
    one must watch over shoulder
    for death, from behind.

The skeleton crawls
along the abandoned pass,
rattles advancing.

    The souls of the starved
    and the souls that time forgot
    are fuel for fury…

Thousands of soldiers,
the slain of battles, wearied
are screaming for blood…

    Ninety-foot creature
    bites the heads off the captured–
    Drinks from red fountains.

The vicious attacks
will continue as long as
their anger still burns.

    So, GO! Run away!
    Lest the Restless approaches

to vanquish your soul.

Mourn the innocent–
For tonight they will fall to
Gashadokuro.

Zombies

Zombies are reanimated corpses, the loathsome living dead that are the quintessential summation of man's worst fears. In general, today's zombies are portrayed as a result of a contagious infection either by a natural virus or a man-made biochemical agent. They represent the ultimate apocalyptic foe that will usher in the demise of humanity and symbolize the inherent evils of a greedy society and the dangers of conformity.

The earliest legends of zombies date back to the early-1800s in Haiti through enslaved Africans with stories of Vodou witches called *bokor*. They were said to use necromancy to summon and capture *zombie astrals* for the purpose of bringing their clients luck or success. The threat of zombification was even utilized to dissuade slaves from committing suicide. In the early-1900s when the United States occupied Haiti, a number of zombie case studies were revealed on the island and they sparked mass attention.

The popular roots of zombies are traced almost entirely to the 1968 horror classic, *Night of the Living Dead* by George Romero, although they were not called zombies at that time, but ghouls. These slow, relentless monsters with an insatiable hunger stirred the nightmares of horror fans in unimagined ways. For the better part of the following two decades, zombie films grew in popularity. However, it was Japanese video game franchises in the late-90s that gave rise to the zombies that have become so mainstream for the past two decades. Zombies grew faster, more cunning, and harder to control or destroy. While popularity has ebbed just a bit in the past several years, they remain a plentiful trend in modern horror.

As science fights to stay ahead of pandemics and environmental disasters, the buried concerns of a potential zombie apocalypse hover close to the surface of widespread fears. Though they are largely a fictitious device, the science behind zombification has tenuous roots in chemical and psychological possibility, leaving some to believe that zombies may one day be more than our favorite nightmare fuel.

Another Roadkill Revenge Story

Bunker living
ever since they all came home –
Tearing out of their graveyards
    and mausoleums,
Like corroded flightless birds of prey.
Their hunger non-sensical
    and unsatisfied,
Their eyes unfixed and unblinking.
Stench of dirt and desiccation,
Saliva infested with infection
    and mass hysteria.

We didn't see it coming.

What used to be undead deer
became the next human plague,
When Bambi met headfirst with
    that speeding truck.
And who knew deer zombies could
    bite through windshields?

Either extinction or evolution…
Do we die,

or die trying?

We die hiding.

The bunker walls will only
    buy us time until
    we dry up and thin out.
So we wait for death or
    we wait to be eaten–
It's an end, either way.

And the deer shall inherit the earth.

Battle Cry

Drag your decaying limbs
across the parking lot battlefields,
this call goes to all you
Munchers of meninges,
Crunchers of cerebellum,
Frontal lobe feeders
    and
Cortex connoisseurs!

The fight for flesh is levied
in your insatiable favor, and
your mindless pursuit of flavor.
Driven by a scent of decadence
caught in your corroded cilia,
Even as your external meatus
    rots
from your festering face.

Onward, malicious masticators!
For even as we manage
to evade graceless evisceration
We all stop–sooner or later–
    Just
long enough for you
to catch our breath.

Cleansed

Five weeks was all it took
for 100 to become 50k
Quarantined in sealed tents
A horde of gray bodies
and phlegm-tinged air
A minefield of the desperate sick
waiting for vaccines.

2 months was all it took
for 50k to become 230,000
Hospitals transformed into morgues
packed with the corpses of doctors
and nurses and researchers –
A congregation of the Infected
lurching toward the exits.

3 months was all it took
for 230,000 to become a million
For a country to seal its borders
trying to contain the contagion
that morphed into rage,
Festering bodies feasting on
the flesh of their families.

6 months was all it took
for the rampant virus to root,
Destroying the society that
laughed at stories and
scoffed at the warnings and
declared invincibility

when the media went static.

A year was all it took
for the Reek to inherit the earth.
A landscape decomposing and
devouring everything with a pulse,
Rotting under the midday sun,
wiping our insult from her face –

A year was all it took to take us out.